Written by Donald Neal Thurber

Editorial Offices: Glenview, Illinois • Parsippany, New Jersey • New York, New York
Sales Offices: Boston, Massachusetts • Duluth, Georgia • Glenview, Illinois • Coppell, Texas
Sacramento, California • Mesa, Arizona

Acknowledgments

Text

page 56: Barbara J. Winston et al., *Geography: Our Country and Our World*, Grade 4. Glenview: Scott, Foresman and Company, 1991, page 118.

page 72: From *Joke-Away and Riddles Plus* by Robert F. Vitarelli. Special permission granted by Weekly Reader Corporation. Copyright © 1989 by Weekly Reader Corporation.

page 88: "Magical Eraser" from *Where the Sidewalk Ends* by Shel Silverstein. Copyright © 1974 by Evil Eye Music, Inc. Selection reprinted by permission of HarperCollins Publishers and Jonathan Cape Ltd.

page 89: "Moon String" by Beverly J. Letchworth in *Highlights for Children*, March 1988. Used by permission of Highlights for Children, Inc., Columbus, OH. Copyright © 1988.

Illustrations

Cindy Brodie 42, 90; Rondi Collette 35; Laura D'Argo 9, 28, 91; Joshua Gorchov 76; Judith Love 31; Linda Hawkins 92; Gary Hoover 72, 80, 85; Yoshi Miyaki 19, 55, 70 (bottom), 71; Deb Morse 68; James Needham 86; Kate Pagni (calligraphy) 36, 70, 71; Gary Phillips 73, 75; Cindy Salans-Rosenheim 34, Lauren Scheuer 57, 93; Jeff Severn 38, 53; Georgia Shola 6, 27, 50, 66, 82; Ken Spieling 20, 21, 74; Carol Stutz 56, (lettering) 16, 18, 19, 30, 40, 52, 54; Susan Swan 12, 17 (right), 89; Andrea Tachiera 32, 81; Darcy Whitehead 3, 4, 5, 8, 11, 12, 16, 17, 22, 23, 60, 61, 63, 70 (top), 87

Photographs

Every effort has been made to secure permission and provide appropriate credit for photographic material. The publisher deeply regrets any omission and pledges to correct errors called to its attention in subsequent editions.

Unless otherwise acknowledged, all photographs are the property of Scott Foresman, a division of Pearson Education.

Photo locators denoted as follows: Top (T), Center (C), Bottom (B), Left (L), Right (R), Background (Bkgd).

10 ©H. Ross/Robertstock; 14 SuperStock; 19 SuperStock; 65 Ndakinna Wilderness project/ ©James Bruchac; 77 ©United Feature Syndicate, Inc./United Media

D'Nealian® Handwriting is a registered trademark of Donald Neal Thurber.

ISBN: 0-328-21204-0

Copyright © 2008 Pearson Education, Inc.
All rights reserved. Printed in the United States of America.

This publication is protected by Copyright, and permission should be obtained from the publisher prior to any prohibited reproduction, storage in a retrieval system, or transmission in any form or by any means, electronic, mechanical, photocopying, recording, or otherwise. For information regarding permission(s), write to: Permissions Department, Scott Foresman, 1900 East Lake Avenue, Glenview Illinois 60025.

4 5 6 7 8 9 10 11 V064 16 15 14 13 12 11

Table of Contents

Unit One Reviewing Manuscript Letters

- 6 Reviewing Lower-case Manuscript Letters
- 7 Reviewing Capital Manuscript Letters
- 8 Reviewing Numbers
- 9 Making a Bookplate
- 10 Writing a Message

Unit Two Writing Cursive Letters

- 12 Writing Cursive lL, hH, and kK
- 13 Writing Cursive tT, iI, and uU
- 14 Writing Cursive eE, jJ, and pP
- 15 Practice
- 16 Review
- 17 Evaluation
- 18 Is Your Writing Legible?
- 20 Using Proofreading Marks
- 22 Timed Writing
- 23 Writing a Language Arts Test
- 26 Writing Cursive aA, dD, and cC
- 27 Writing Cursive nN, mM, and xX
- 28 Writing Cursive gG, yY, and qQ
- 29 Practice
- 30 Review
- 31 Evaluation
- 32 Letter Size and Proportion
- 34 Making a Business Card
- 35 Solving a Crossword Puzzle
- 36 Fun with Handwriting: Show-off Writing
- 37 Writing Cursive oO, wW, and bB
- 38 Joining Sidestroke Letters
- 39 Practice
- 40 Review
- 41 Evaluation
- 42 Letter Form
- 44 Timed Writing
- 45 Writing a Math Test
- 48 Writing Cursive vV and zZ
- 49 Writing Cursive sS, rR, and fF
- 50 Joining Sidestroke Letters
- 51 Practice
- 52 Review
- 53 Evaluation
- 54 Letter Slant
- 56 Timed Writing
- 57 Writing a Language Arts Test
- 60 Fun with Handwriting: Awards

Unit Three Applying Handwriting Skills

- **62** Writing the Time
- **63** Making a Schedule
- **64** Writing Addresses
- **65** Writing a Postcard
- **66** Writing Measurements
- **67** Writing a Recipe
- **68** Writing Ordinal Numbers
- **70** Fun with Handwriting: Calligraphy
- **72** Fun with Handwriting: Riddles
- **73** Letter, Word, and Sentence Spacing
- **75** Timed Writing
- **76** Writing an Announcement
- **77** Writing Punctuation Marks
- **78** Writing a Journal Entry
- **80** Writing Proper Nouns
- **81** Making Signs
- **82** Writing Dates
- **83** Keeping an Assignment Book
- **84** Timed Writing
- **85** Fun with Handwriting: Fantastic Letters
- **86** Writing Titles
- **87** Writing a List of Favorite Books
- **88** Writing a Poem
- **90** Making a Poster
- **91** Writing a Thank-you Note
- **92** Timed Writing
- **93** Writing a Science Test
- **96** Index

Unit One

Reviewing Manuscript Letters

Reviewing Lower-case Manuscript Letters

On a sheet of paper, write a row of each lower-case letter.

a a a a	j j j j	s s s s
b b b b	k k k k	t t t t
c c c c	l l l l	u u u u
d d d d	m m m m	v v v v
e e e e	n n n n	w w w w
f f f f	o o o o	x x x x
g g g g	p p p p	y y y y
h h h h	q q q q	z z z z
i i i i	r r r r	

Tim's class watched special events at school and went on field trips. Number your paper from 1 to 5. Write the class's favorites in manuscript.

1. **harmonica players**
2. **dancing puppets**
3. **wild animal trainers**
4. **backstage at a theater**
5. **tour of old airplanes**

6

Reviewing Capital Manuscript Letters

On a sheet of paper, write a row of each capital letter.

A A A A   J J J J   S S S S
B B B B   K K K K   T T T T
C C C C   L L L L   U U U U
D D D D   M M M M   V V V V
E E E E   N N N N   W W W W
F F F F   O O O O   X X X X
G G G G   P P P P   Y Y Y Y
H H H H   Q Q Q Q   Z Z Z Z
I I I I   R R R R

Stephanie's class always plans a special event for Friday. On Thursday, they put a reminder card on the bulletin board. Number your paper from 1 to 5. Write the reminders below in manuscript.

1. **Furry Visitors Hour**
2. **Invention Time**
3. **Green Eggs Day**
4. **Musical Showtime**
5. **Health Nut Snack**

Reviewing Numbers

On a sheet of paper, write a row of each number.

When you write a number of more than three figures, use a comma [,] to separate hundreds from thousands.

Jackie hopes she will attend these festivals someday. She looked up how many miles she would have to travel from her home in Detroit.

Number your paper from 1 to 3. Write Jackie's notes.

1. **716 miles to Milwaukee**
2. **1,211 miles to Cheyenne**
3. **1,747 miles to Albuquerque**

Making a Bookplate

Clarence reads and collects adventure books. When he lends one to a friend, he pastes a bookplate inside the front cover. He found that the bookplate is a reminder for people to return the book. Look at his bookplate below.

On a sheet of paper, draw a space about the size of Clarence's bookplate. Then copy his bookplate or create one of your own. Use manuscript writing. Plan ahead and adjust your writing to fit the space. Add artwork if you like.

Writing a Message

Hiro lives near the ocean. When he sees large boats in the harbor, he becomes curious about the distant lands they go to. He decided to try to communicate with someone far away, so he wrote a message, put it in a bottle, and threw it into the ocean.

Read Hiro's message below. He planned his writing so that there was enough space between words and sentences.

August 10, 200__

Hello!
   My name is Hiro Yamamoto. I am 10 years old and I live at 349 Noyes Street, San Diego, CA 92109. I like to make model ships and learn about foreign lands.
   Please write and tell me where you found this message.

                    Sincerely,
                      Hiro

On your paper, draw a space about the size of the one above. In manuscript, write a message that you would like someone in another country to read. Leave enough space between words and sentences. Remember to write in a straight line if your paper doesn't have writing lines.

Look at the message you wrote. Is there enough space between words and sentences?

Writing Cursive lL, hH, and kK

On a sheet of paper, write a row of each lower-case letter. Be sure to
- touch the top line with the uphill stroke.
- keep the loops open.

Notice where the capital letters **L, H,** and **K** touch the top line. Write a row of each letter.

Capital Letter Link-ups

Remember that **L** and **K** join the letters that follow them. Trace the joined letters in the box with your finger.

H does not join the letter that follows it. Finger trace **Ha**.

Number your paper from 1 to 2. Write the following phrases.

1. John Hancock Lookout Deck
2. Hillside Lake Kite Day

12

Writing Cursive tT, iI, and uU

On a sheet of paper, write a row of each lower-case letter. Be sure to
- cross **t** and dot **i**.
- make **i** and **u** half as tall as **t**.

Notice where the capital letters **T, I,** and **U** touch the top line. Write a row of each letter.

Capital Letter Link-ups

Remember that **I** and **U** join the letters that follow them. Trace the joined letters in the box with your finger.

T does not join the letter that follows it. Finger trace **Th**.

Number your paper from 1 to 2. Write the following phrases.

1. Union Train Museum

2. Island School Talent Show

13

Writing Cursive eE, jJ, and pP

On a sheet of paper, write a row of each lower-case letter. Be sure to
- dot **j.**
- keep the loop open in **e.**

Notice where the capital letters **E, J,** and **P** touch the top line. Write a row of each letter.

 Capital Letter Link-ups
Remember that **E** and **J** join the letters that follow them. Trace the joined letters in the box with your finger.

P does not join the letter that follows it. Finger trace **Pa.**

Number your paper from 1 to 2. Write the following names of events.

1. Early American Toys Display
2. Jacob Lawrence Art Project

Practice

Some letter combinations appear more often than others. On a sheet of paper, write a row of each pair of letters. Be sure to
- write **l** and **k** with a loop.
- write **t** without a loop.

Number your paper from 1 to 5. Now write the proper names and sentences below. Be sure to write **l** and **k** with a loop. Write **t** without a loop.

1. Wilkie Tower
2. Adler College
3. A guide led us as we walked through the tower.
4. We laughed and talked in the crowded elevator.
5. Some people relaxed near the fountain on the ground level.

Review

Remember that you join capital letters **L, K, I, U, E,** and **J** to the lower-case letters that follow them. Number a sheet of paper from 1 to 14. Write these names.

1. **Luellen**   2. **Kyle**   3. **Ileana**

4. **Ursula**   5. **Eloise**   6. **Jake**

Remember that you do not join capital letters **H, T,** and **P** to the lower-case letters that follow them. Write the names of these cities.

7. **Hopewell**   8. **Tupelo**   9. **El Paso**

Spot a Problem

Tell why the cursive words below are hard to read.

like
like
10. _____

pull
puee
11. _____

Now write **like** and **pull** so that they are easy to read.

12. _____   13. _____

Write the following phrase. Make sure your tall letters touch the top line.

14. **from the top of a tall building**

16

Evaluation

Read the hints. Then write the paragraph below on a sheet of paper. Make your handwriting easy to read.

Hints for Clear Handwriting
- Join lower-case letters.
- Make your tall letters touch the top line.

Our class went to the top of the Hancock Building. The day was clear. We watched sailboats on the sparkling lake and cars snaking down crowded streets. The view was great in every direction!

Check Your Handwriting

Is your handwriting improving? Use the marks below to check the paragraph you wrote.

In the first sentence, **circle** lower-case letters that are not joined.

In the second sentence, **write a check mark above** tall letters that do not touch the top line.

On your paper, write the marks and the number of times you wrote them.

○ _____   √ _____

Low scores mean your handwriting is easy to read!

Is Your Writing Legible?

Is your handwriting legible or does it look like a secret code? A secret code is impossible to figure out without any clues. Make sure you give your reader all the clues when you write. Check for the following points in your handwriting.

Letter Size and Proportion

Your writing will be easy to read if your letters are the correct size. Look at the letters at the right. The small letters are half the size of the tall letters. The tall letters touch the top line. Letters with descenders go below the bottom line.

Number a sheet of paper from 1 to 3. Then write your name. Concentrate on making your letters the correct size.

1. _____

Letter Form

Can you read the word below? The word is **outing.** Why is it hard to read?

Write **outing** correctly. Remember to close **o,** cross **t,** and dot **i.**

2. _____

Write the name of one of your classmates. Concentrate on forming your letters correctly.

3. _____

Now ask that classmate to read the name. Does he or she think it's legible?

Letter Slant

Your handwriting will be easy to read if you slant all your letters the same way. Don't worry if your letters slant in a different direction from your classmate's. Number a sheet of paper from 1 to 4. Write the name of your school.

1. _____

Look at the words you wrote. Then look at the examples below. Write the word or phrase that describes your slant.

right   left   up and down

2. _____

Letter and Word Spacing

Be sure that you have the right amount of spacing between letters and words. Don't crowd letters too closely together. Leave more space between words than between letters in a word. Write the question below.

Where are you in the group photo?

3. _____

Look at the examples below. Then look at the question you wrote. Write the word or phrase that describes the spacing in your handwriting.

even   too close

too far apart

4. _____

Using Proofreading Marks

In the paragraph below, Rita used proofreading marks to show how she wanted to correct her copy. The proofreading marks and what they mean are shown at the right. Notice how Rita corrected her copy. Look at the position of each mark.

Proofreading Marks

≡ Make a capital letter.
∧ Add a word or words.
(sp) Correct the spelling.
⊙ Add a period.
? Add a question mark.
! Add an exclamation mark.
℮ Take out a word or words.

> Do you like stories?
> what I like
> Mysteries are ∧ best. I
> (sp) red one to my ~~my~~   (sp) read
>   really
> sister. she was ∧ scared!

On a sheet of paper, write a neat final copy of Rita's paragraph. Make the corrections shown by the proofreading marks. You do not have to skip lines. Use cursive writing.

Look at what you wrote. Did you make all the corrections? Does your writing look neat?

20

Read the paragraph below. Notice the mistakes. Use the proofreading marks on page 20 to show how the paragraph should be corrected.

The book is abot Cam—a detective with the a great memory. She new there should 34 bones in the dinosaur's skeleton. but she saw only 31

On your paper, write the paragraph as a final copy. Make the corrections shown by the proofreading marks. You do not have to skip lines. Use cursive writing.

Read what you wrote. Did you make all the corrections? Does the paragraph make sense?

Timed Writing

Tom's teacher gave the students four minutes before the end of class to copy the instructions for an assignment. Read the assignment below.

> *Language Assignment*
>
> Look through newspapers and magazines. Cut out pictures of three animals you think are interesting. Write three sentences. Tell why you liked each animal. Leave enough space after each sentence so that you can paste the animal's picture near it. Turn in the paper tomorrow.

When you have to write quickly, use these tips.
- First, read what you have to copy. Think about how you can write it in a shorter form and still include all the important information.
- Use manuscript or cursive, whichever you write faster.
- When you write, skip words that are not important.

On a separate sheet of paper, write Tom's assignment. Time your writing. Use a clock, a timer, or have a friend time you. Stop writing when four minutes are up.

Now read what you wrote. Do you understand the assignment? Did you remember to write when it is due?

Writing for a Test

Good handwriting helps you do your best when you write for a test.
Good handwriting makes your answers easier to read.
Good handwriting helps you communicate your ideas more clearly.
Good handwriting helps you answer test questions within a specified amount of time.

Getting Ready
- Read the test prompt carefully.
- Think about what you want to write.

Writing a Response
- Plan your writing by organizing your ideas.
- Express your ideas clearly and completely.
  Support your ideas with details or examples.
  Choose words that will help others understand what you mean.
  Use correct grammar, spelling, punctuation, and paragraphs.
- Use your best handwriting.
  Letters should not be too close together or too far apart.
  Letters should be the correct size and proportion to fit the space given.
- Review and edit your writing.
  Use proofreading marks to make corrections or erase carefully and rewrite.

Everyone has tried something new at one time or another. Think about a time you tried something new. Now write a story about that time.

I remember a time wen I (sp) When was in third grade I had never been to a baseball game before. Can you believe that?

23

Here is a writing prompt and Marisa's answer.

> Everyone has jobs or chores. Think about one of your jobs or chores. Now explain why you do your job or chore.

> Last year we got a cat named Whiskers and he is white with black paws and he is very ~~frendly~~. My little sisters job is to ~~feed~~ whiskers every day in the morning. My job is to wash the dishes after dinner every night and in the morning I make my bed before I go to school. If I'm late for school then I make my bed when I get home. I like helping at home.

Look at how Marisa wrote her answer.   Yes   No
- Is there the same amount of space between each of the letters in her words?
- Did she use correct letter size and proportion?
- Did she fix mistakes carefully?
- Did she organize her ideas well?
- Did she support her ideas with examples or details?

What letters do not have the correct spacing, size, or proportion? Write the words on a separate piece of paper under the heads *Space, Size, Proportion.* Which ideas do not support Marisa's answer? Write them. Which sentence should go first in the paragraph? Write it.

24

Now use a separate piece of paper to write a response to the same prompt that Marisa used.

Check your handwriting.   Yes   No

Number your paper 1 to 5. Answer the questions.
1. Is there the same amount of space between each of the letters in your words?
2. Did you use correct letter size and proportion?
3. Did you fix mistakes carefully?
4. Did you organize your ideas well?
5. Did you support your ideas with examples or details?

Draw a line under the sentence you wrote best.

Writing Cursive aA, dD, and cC

On a sheet of paper, write a row of each lower-case letter.
Be sure to
- close **a** and **d**.
- keep **c** open.

Notice where the capital letters **A, D,** and **C** touch the top line. Write a row of each letter.

 Capital Letter Link-ups
Remember that **A** and **C** join the letters that follow them. Trace the joined letters in the box with your finger.

D does not join the letter that follows it. Finger trace **Dr.**

Number your paper from 1 to 2. Write the following names of events.

1. Young American Authors Day
2. Drummers and Dancers Concert

Writing Cursive nN, mM, and xX

Imagine that there is a dotted line halfway between each of the lines on your paper. Write a row of each lower-case letter. Make **n, m,** and **x** touch the imaginary midline.

Notice that capital letters **N, M,** and **X** have the same beginning stroke. Write a row of each letter.

Capital Letter Link-ups

Remember that **N** and **M** join the letters that follow them. Trace the joined letters in the box with your finger.

X does not join the letter that follows it. Finger trace **Xa.**

Number your paper from 1 to 2. Write the following names of events.

1. Newport News Music Festival
2. Lake Xochimilco Mural Opening

Writing Cursive gG, yY, and qQ

On a sheet of paper, write a row of each lower-case letter. Be sure to
- swing the bottom loop of **g** and **y** to the left.
- swing the bottom loop of **q** to the right.

Notice that capital letters **Q** and **Y** start near the top line. **G** starts at the bottom line. Write a row of each letter.

 Capital Letter Link-ups

Remember that **Y** and **Q** join the letters that follow them. Trace the joined letters in the box with your finger.

G does not join the letter that follows it. Finger trace **Ga**.

Number your paper from 1 to 2. Write the following phrases.

1. Grafton Square Yoyo Players
2. Recycling Quart and Gallon Bottles

Practice

Some letter combinations appear more often than others. On a sheet of paper, write a row of each pair of letters. Be sure to
- swing the loops of **g** and **y** to the left.
- close **a** and **d**.

Number your paper from 1 to 5. Write the proper nouns and the sentences below. Be sure to swing the loops of **g** and **y** to the left. Close **a** and **d**.

1. Dance Theater
2. Ridgeway Woods
3. Yesterday we went to an outdoor concert at Edgewater Park.
4. Six children dressed as mice danced over the gray bridge.
5. Quincy didn't budge during the performance.

Review

Remember that you join capital letters **A, C, N, M, Y,** and **Q** to the lower-case letters that follow them. Number a sheet of paper from 1 to 14. Write these names.

1. **Audrey**
2. **Cooper**
3. **Nancy**
4. **Miguel**
5. **Yolanda**
6. **Quon**

Remember that you do not join capital letters **D, X,** and **G** to the lower-case letters that follow them. Write the names of these cities.

7. **Dexter**
8. **Xenia**
9. **Grundy**

Spot a Problem

Tell why the cursive words below are hard to read.

voices

voices

10. _____

fiddle

fiddle

11. _____

Now write **voices** and **fiddle** so that they are easy to read.

12. _____   13. _____

Write the following phrase. Make sure your closed letters are properly formed.

14. **a quartet singing a melody**

Evaluation

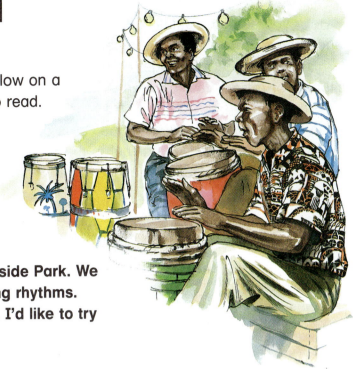

Read the hints. Then write the paragraph below on a sheet of paper. Make your handwriting easy to read.

Hints for Clear Handwriting
- Close letters **a** and **d**.
- Use only cursive letters.

On Monday we went on a field trip to Riverside Park. We watched a group of drummers playing exciting rhythms. Afterwards, we took turns playing the drums. I'd like to try that again someday.

Check Your Handwriting

Is your handwriting improving? Use the marks below to check the paragraph you wrote.

In the first sentence, **circle** every **a** and **d** that is not closed.

In the second sentence, **write a check mark above** every letter that is not in cursive.

On your paper, write the marks and the number of times you wrote them.

○ _____   √ _____

Low scores mean your handwriting is easy to read!

31

Letter Size and Proportion

Have you seen the small chairs and tables for kindergarten children? In the upper grades, the size of the furniture changes to fit bigger children. Make sure you change, or adjust, your handwriting to fit the size of the writing space.

On a sheet of paper, draw name cards about the size of the ones below. Write the names on the cards. Adjust your writing to fit each space. Use manuscript writing.

Missie

Danica

Benny filled in a name tag for his backpack. Some of his numbers bumped into letters with descenders. On a sheet of paper, make a name tag form like the one below. Copy the information from Benny's name tag in the form. Make sure each letter has its own space.

This belongs to

Name: *Benny King*

Address: *5580 S. 79th St.*
Chicago, IL 60637

Did you plan well? Is your writing too big, too small, or just about right?

To make sure your letters are the right size, make your tall letters and numbers touch the top lines. Make your small letters half the size of your tall letters.

Look at the letters on the chalkboard at the right. Some of them are the answers to the letter riddles below. Number a sheet of paper from 1 to 4. Write each riddle and its answer in cursive.

1. **Which letter can you drink?**

2. **Which letter is a bird?**

3. **Which letter stings?**

A teacher and a student wrote the names of two special days at their school. The student used student proportion, but the teacher used adult proportion. Notice that the student's tall letters touch the top line, but the teacher's do not. In both examples the small letters are half the size of the tall letters. This means that both handwriting examples are in correct proportion.

student proportion

Earth Day

adult proportion

Arbor Day

Now write the words below in adult proportion. Make your small letters half the size of the tall letters.

4. **Spaulding School Fun Fair**

Making a Business Card

Ruben wants to earn money by baby-sitting and dog-walking in his spare time. When he tells people that he is available, he hands them business cards that he made so they will remember him.

Look at Ruben's business card. Notice that he wrote the kinds of jobs he wants in larger letters. He wrote the rest of the information in smaller letters.

Baby-sitting   Dog-walking

Call Ruben Morales   555-6193

Weekdays, 4:15 – 7:30 p.m.
Saturdays and Sundays, all afternoon

On a sheet of paper, draw a space about the size of the one below. Create your own business card. Use manuscript writing. Write the job you want in bigger letters. Write the rest of the information in smaller letters. Adjust your handwriting to fit the space.

Look at the card you wrote. If you were going to write a real business card, would you need to change anything?

Maintaining Manuscript

Solving a Crossword Puzzle

Patti's grandpa made her a birthday card with a crossword puzzle. When she solved it, she found that the words described *her*.

On a sheet of paper, solve the crossword puzzle below. Use manuscript writing.

Clues

Down:

1. She will have a *jolly* birthday.
2. She wants to be *a person who puts out flames.*
4. She makes people *giggle.*
5. She likes to *fool* me.

Across:

3. She is a *wonderful* granddaughter.
6. Her favorite sport is *splashing.*
7. She is *five plus five* years old today.

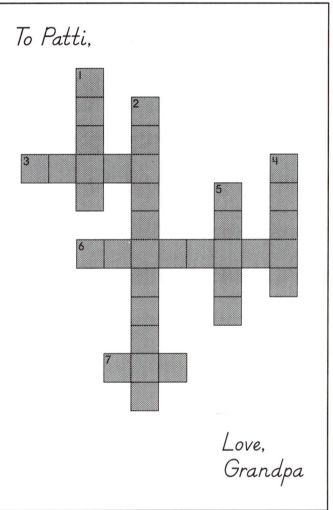

Maintaining Manuscript

Fun with Handwriting: Show-off Writing

Big
Bigger
BIGGEST

Just by looking at the way those words are written, you can understand what they mean. Pick some words from the list below or think of your own. Then let your imagination go.

On a separate sheet of paper, create your own word pictures. Write the letters so they show the meaning of the word. Would manuscript or cursive handwriting show the meaning better? Would capital or lower-case letters be better?

zero	giraffe	ladder	bubble
butterfly	basketball	tiny	sneeze
snake	strong	bumpy	shadow

Writing Cursive oO, wW, and bB

On a sheet of paper, write a row of each lower-case letter. Be sure to
- close **o**.
- keep the loop open on **b**.

Notice that capital letters **O** and **B** start at the top line, while **W** starts just below it. Write a row of each letter.

Capital Letter Link-ups

Remember that **O, W,** and **B** do not join the letters that follow them.

Trace the letter groups in the box with your finger.

On We Br

Number your paper from 1 to 2. Write the following names of events.

1. *Indoor Obstacle Bike Race*
2. *"What will I be?" Day*

Joining Sidestroke Letters

Look at letters **o** and **n** at the right. Now look at the joined letters **on**. Notice that
- before joining, the beginning stroke of **n** touches the bottom line.
- after joining, the beginning stroke of **n** does not touch the bottom line.

o n on

When you join letters **o, w,** and **b** to other letters, do not touch the bottom line.

ot wh br

Number your paper from 1 to 8. Write the words and sentences below.

1. *one*
2. *work*
3. *oboe*
4. *who*
5. *wobble*
6. *bobber*

7. *Wesley whispered to the watchful woodchuck.*

8. *Belinda ate berries under the branches of a big birch tree.*

Practice

Some letter combinations appear more often than others. On a sheet of paper, write a row of each pair of letters. Be sure to
- keep the loop open on **b**.
- close **o**.
- make **o** and **w** half as tall as **b**.

Number your paper from 1 to 6. Now write the names of the places and sentences below. Be sure your small letters are half the size of your tall letters.

1. Coulee Dam
2. Pebble Beach
3. Bill daydreams about what he'll be and where he'll go someday.
4. He wonders what he'll be able to do.
5. He thinks about flying a blimp.
6. He imagines touring London while riding a double-decker bus.

Review

Remember that you do not join capital cursive letters **O**, **W**, and **B** to the lower-case letters that follow them. Number a sheet of paper from 1 to 14. Write these names.

1. **Beth**
2. **Olivia**
3. **Willow**
4. **William**
5. **Barry**
6. **Orville**

Remember to make your small letters half the size of your tall letters. Write the names of these American towns.

7. **Woodbury**
8. **Boonton**
9. **Ottawa**

Spot a Problem

Tell why the cursive words below are hard to read.

wish

hope

10. _____
11. _____

Now write **wish** and **hope** so that they are easy to read.

12. _____
13. _____

Write the following phrase. Use a sidestroke to join **o**, **w**, and **b** to the letters that follow them.

14. **winning a blue ribbon**

40

Evaluation

Read the hints. Then write the paragraph below on a sheet of paper. Make your handwriting easy to read.

Hints for Clear Handwriting
- Close **o**.
- Keep the loop open on **b**.

Win always notices a sculpture of a little angel on a nearby church. It's made of stone, but it looks soft and chubby. At home, Win makes her own angels out of clay. First she shapes a face and a small body. Then she adds wings.

Check Your Handwriting

Is your handwriting improving? Use the marks below to check the paragraph you wrote.

In the first sentence, **circle** every **o** that is not closed.

In the second sentence, **write a check mark near** every **b** that does not have a loop.

On your paper, write the marks and the number of times you wrote them.

○ _____   √ _____

Low scores mean your handwriting is easy to read!

41

Letter Form

It would be hard to ride a bicycle with parts that are not made correctly. It is also hard to read handwriting when the letters are not formed correctly. When you write, make sure letters like **l** and **h** have loops. Cross **t** and dot **i** and **j.**

Jason rode his new bicycle to the library. He wanted the books listed below, but he could not find them on the shelves. Number a sheet of paper from 1 to 5. Write the titles and authors below. Remember to underline titles of books.

1. <u>**How to Speak Clearly**</u> **by Whujuh Sey**

2. <u>**Yummy Meals**</u> **by Aunt Eder**

3. <u>**101 Excuses**</u> **by I. M. Lion**

4. <u>**Scary Stories**</u> **by Yell N. Holler**

5. <u>**My Life in the Circus**</u> **by Akro Batt**

Look at what you wrote. Did you form your letters correctly?

Letters like the ones at the right are easy to read because they are formed correctly. Cursive **e** is open but **i** is not. Cursive **l** has a loop but **t** does not.

Jason was able to find books about what he likes to do in his spare time. Number a sheet of paper from 1 to 5. Then write the topics of Jason's books.

1. **doodling and painting**

2. **acting in skits**

3. **collecting fingerprints**

Make sure the bottom loops on your descender letters swing in the correct direction. Look at the letters at the right. Cursive **g** and **y** have bottom loops that swing to the left, but **q** has a bottom loop that swings to the right.

Write the sentences below. Think about how to form each letter as you write it.

4. **Jason stopped for a while at a display of holograms.**

5. **Then he checked out the books and rode quickly home.**

Look at your writing. Are the letters formed correctly?

Timed Writing

After choir practice, Mrs. Robinson asked Sheila to give her dad a message. When Sheila got home, she quickly wrote the message down so she wouldn't forget it. The message was on the table when Sheila's dad got home from work. Below, read what Mrs. Robinson told Sheila.

"Sheila, you know that your dad is organizing a bake sale. Would you tell him that I will not be able to help at the sale on Saturday? I have to go out of town that day, but I'll drop off my bread on Friday. Thanks for your help!"

Use these tips when you write a message for someone else.
- Include important names, dates, and events.
- Use manuscript or cursive, whichever is faster.
- Write in complete sentences so that the message will be easy for the reader to understand.

Decide what parts of Mrs. Robinson's message are important to write down. Then write the message in either manuscript or cursive on another sheet of paper. Time your writing. Use a clock, a timer, or have a friend time you. Stop writing when four minutes are up.

Now read what you wrote. Did you write down the names, days, and events?

Writing a Math Test

Good handwriting helps you do well on math tests. Good handwriting makes your numbers and words easy to read.

Getting Ready
- Read the test question carefully.
- Be sure you understand what the question is asking you to do.

Finding the Rule

> Fill in the missing output number in the table.
> What is the rule?

- Look at the numbers in the input boxes. Figure out what operation you use to change them to output numbers.
- Tell the rule for changing the input numbers.
- Use your best handwriting.
  The size of your handwriting should fit the space in the table.
  All your numbers and letters should slant in the same direction.

Input	Output
8	32
9	36
10	40
11	*44*

Multiply by 4.

- Review and edit your writing. Use proofreading marks to make corrections or erase carefully and rewrite.

45

Miguel completed the input/output table below. Then he wrote the rule.

Fill in the missing output number in the table. Write the rule.

Input	Output
3	9
4	16
5	25
6	36

Multiply each input numbr by itself.

Look at how Miguel solved the problem.
- Did he adjust his handwriting to fit the table?
- Do his letters and numbers slant the same way?
- Is his handwriting easy to read?

Yes   No

Which letters and number do not have the correct slant?
Which words are spelled incorrectly?
Write the words on a separate piece of paper under the heads *Slant* and *Spelling*.

46

Now you find the missing numbers in the table below. On a separate piece of paper, write the rule.

Fill in the missing numbers in the table.
What is the rule?

Input	Output
6	18
	21
8	24
9	

Check your handwriting.   Yes   No

Number your paper from 1 – 4. Write your answers.
1. Did you adjust your handwriting to fit the table?
2. Do your letters and numbers slant
   the same way?
3. Is your handwriting easy to read?
4. Did you fix mistakes carefully?

Circle the number you wrote best.

47

Writing Cursive vV and zZ

Imagine that there is a dotted line halfway between each of the lines on your paper. Write a row of each lower-case letter. Make **v** and **z** touch the imaginary midline.

Notice that capital letters **V** and **Z** start below the top line. Write a row of each letter.

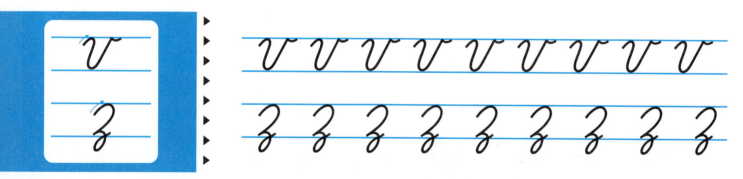

Capital Letter Link-ups
Remember that **Z** joins the letters that follow it. Trace the joined letters in the box with your finger.

V does not join the letter that follows it. Finger trace **Vo**.

Number your paper from 1 to 3. Write the following names of events.

1. Riverview Cavern Visit
2. Vandalia Zoo Trip
3. Crazy Questions Quiz Show

Writing Cursive sS, rR, and fF

On a sheet of paper, write a row of each lower-case letter. Be sure to
- keep **r** open.
- close **s**.

Notice that capital **F** has three strokes. Write a row of each letter.

 Capital Letter Link-ups

Remember that **R** joins the letter that follows it. Trace the joined letters in the box with your finger.

S and **F** do not join the letters that follow them. Finger trace **Sa** and **Fr**.

Ro
Sa Fr

Number your paper from 1 to 2. Write these events.

1. *East Rumford Science Fair*
2. *Submarine Tour Field Trip*

49

Joining Sidestroke Letters

Look at letters **o, w, b,** and **v** at the right. They end with sidestrokes. These strokes do not touch the bottom line.

Use a sidestroke when you join **o, w, b,** and **v** to other letters.

o w b v

of wr bu ve

Number your paper from 1 to 8. Write the words and sentences below.

1. out
2. way
3. bobcat
4. went
5. voter
6. volley

7. Vanessa viewed a very lovely valley.

8. Oscar opened oodles of oysters over by the ocean.

50

Practice

Some letter combinations appear more often than others. On a sheet of paper, write a row of each pair of letters. Be sure to
- write **f** and **h** with loops.
- close **s.**

ve ve ve ve ve ve ve ve ve
sh sh sh sh sh sh sh sh sh
fr fr fr fr fr fr fr fr fr fr

Number your paper from 1 to 5. Now write the proper nouns and the sentences below. Be sure to keep the loops open in **f** and **h** and close **s.**

1. Fishing Derby
2. Harvest Festival
3. Would you like to have some outdoor creatures as friends?
4. If you have an old wooden tub, you can build a fishpond.
5. Add fresh water, plants, and shells, if you wish.
6. Birds, frogs, and snails love ponds!

Review

Remember that you join capital letters **Z** and **R** to the lower-case letters that follow them. Number a sheet of paper from 1 to 14. Write these names.

1. **Zondra**
2. **Rosetta**
3. **Rafael**
4. **Roger**
5. **Zeb**
6. **Zeke**

Remember that you do not join capital letters **V, S,** and **F** to the lower-case letters that follow them. Write the names of these places.

7. **Sun Valley**
8. **Stonington**
9. **Fairhaven**

Spot a Problem

Tell why the cursive words below are hard to read.

sister

sister

10. _____

remember

remember

11. _____

Now write **sister** and **remember** so that they are easy to read.

12. _____   13. _____

Write the following phrase. Make sure your small letters are half the size of your tall letters.

14. **rain drizzling on the soft ground**

52

Evaluation

Read the hints. Then write the paragraph below on a sheet of paper. Make your handwriting easy to read.

Hints for Clear Handwriting
- Close **s**.
- Write **f** with two loops.

    Every spring Uncle Russell and I start our garden. We plant colorful flowers, cauliflower, and other vegetables. But we're always chasing away hungry rabbits that eat the plants. Rabbits are fun to watch. How can we have a garden and rabbits too?

Check Your Handwriting

Is your handwriting improving? Use the marks below to check the paragraph you wrote.

In the first sentence, **circle** every **s** that is not closed.

In the second sentence, **write a check mark next to** every **f** that does not have loops.

On your paper, write the number of marks you made.

Low scores mean your handwriting is easy to read!

53

Letter Slant

Imagine what a tug-of-war would be like if the people on your side pulled in different directions. They would probably bump into each other. When you write, slant your letters in the same direction so they don't bump into each other. Study the sentences below. Number a sheet of paper from 1 to 4. Then copy the sentence that tells how your writing slants.

1. _____

Kate used many punctuation marks in a story she wrote about how she played when she was younger. Copy the following sentences from her story. Slant your letters and punctuation marks in the same direction.

2. **Imagine what we could make out of these huge boxes, some blankets, and a rope!**

3. **Let's make holes in the boxes for doors and windows.**

4. **We'll call it the "Enchanted Towers."**

Remember that numbers must slant in the same direction as the rest of your handwriting.

The children in Kate's story imagined that everything was larger than it really was. Number a sheet of paper from 1 to 3. Then write the following phrases from her story.

1. **200 feet high**

2. **10,000 mosquitoes**

3. **110 degrees**

To make your handwriting easy to read, keep your tall letters from bumping into letters with descenders. Look at the descender letters and tall letters in the paragraph below. Each letter is in its own space. On your paper, copy what Kate wrote in her journal.

Today my imagination came in handy. This morning I made up a riddle. In school, I wrote a story, and on the way home, I daydreamed about being an inventor.

Timed Writing

Do you ever read a textbook chapter and then forget what you read? If you take short notes, you will probably remember more.

Use these tips to take notes from a textbook.
- First, read through the part you are assigned.
- Go back and write down important facts, dates, and definitions. Use manuscript or cursive, whichever you write faster.
- Write legibly so you can read the notes at a later time.

Read through the paragraph about steam power below. On a separate sheet of paper, write three or four notes about what you read. Time your reading and note-taking. Use a clock, a timer, or have a friend time you. Stop when four minutes are up.

The coming of steam power. Inventors in England had been working on the steam engine for many years. Finally, in 1769, an Englishman named James Watt built a steam engine that worked well. Now factories could be built anywhere. They no longer needed to be built near water. Steam could be used to power boats, trains, hammers, and pumps.

Can you understand what you wrote? Did you write important facts, dates, and names?

Steam Locomotive

Writing a Language Arts Test

Good handwriting helps you do well on tests. It makes your words easy to read. It helps you communicate your ideas more clearly.

Getting Ready

In a test, you may have to read a passage and answer a question about it by organizing information.
- Read the passage and question carefully.
- Be sure you understand what to do.

Writing a Response
- One test had a passage about water. Here is an example of a web that organizes information from the passage.
- When you write a response, use your best handwriting. Adjust your handwriting to fit the space in the ovals of the web.
- Letters should not be too close together or too far apart.

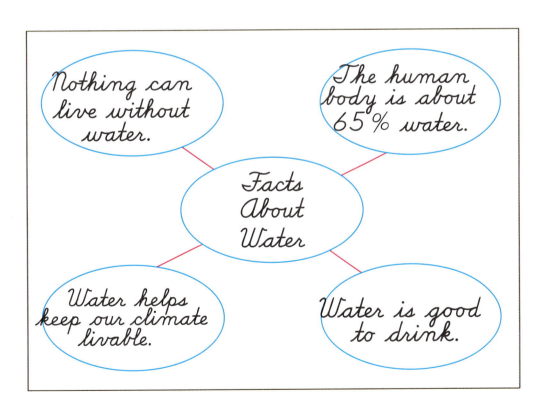

- Review and edit your writing. Use proofreading marks to make corrections or erase carefully and rewrite.

57

Keshia completed a web using the passage below.

Most of Earth's water, about 97 percent, is in the oceans. The remaining 3 percent is fresh water. Most of the fresh water is in glaciers and icecaps. The rest is ground water, rivers, swamps, and lakes. Even though rivers make up a very small percentage of Earth's water, this is where we get most of the water for our everyday use.

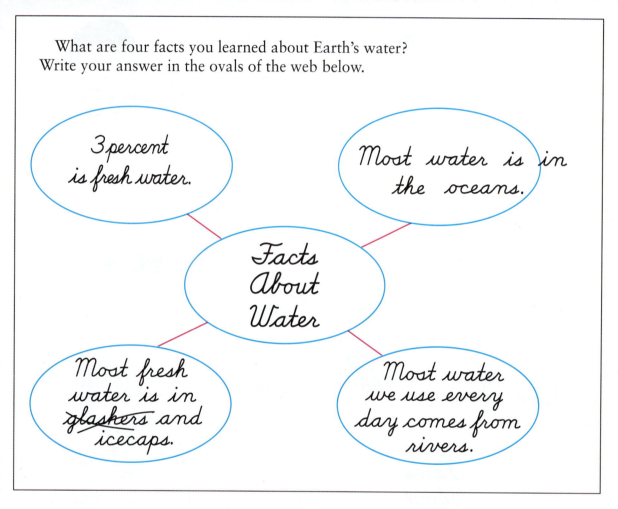

Look at how Keshia answered the question.   Yes   No
- Did she adjust her handwriting to fit the circles?
- Is her handwriting easy to read?
- Did she fix mistakes carefully?

What letters and words are not evenly spaced? On a separate piece of paper, write them under the heading *Space*. Then write correctly the word that is misspelled.

58

On a separate piece of paper, complete a web using the information in the passage below.

Did you know that the same water that existed on Earth millions of years ago is still here today? Thanks to the way water moves in and out of Earth's atmosphere, water is continuously being recycled all around the globe. Earth is a "closed system," like a terrarium. This means that very few of Earth's substances, including water, escape into outer space.

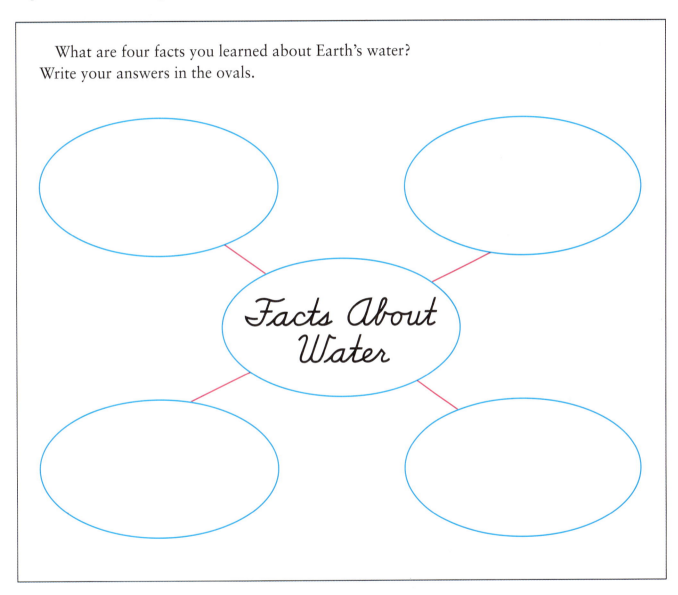

What are four facts you learned about Earth's water? Write your answers in the ovals.

Facts About Water

Check your handwriting.

Number your paper from 1 to 3. Write your answers.
1. Did you adjust your handwriting to fit the space?
2. Is your handwriting easy to read?
3. Did you fix mistakes carefully?

Yes   No

Put a check by the fact you wrote best.

Fun with Handwriting: Awards

On most evenings Leticia could hear her brother trying to play the guitar. When he played his first song, she made him an award. Leticia decided to be creative. She used both manuscript and cursive writing to decorate her award.

On another sheet of paper, make your own award. Be creative!

60

Unit Three

Applying Handwriting Skills

Writing the Time

Jenny has to complete the message at the right. She can write the time in one of three ways shown below. The shortest way is to use numbers. When you use numbers, remember to add a colon [:] to separate the hours from the minutes. Colons are the same size as small lower-case letters.

Chorus practice is today at

quarter past three   *three-fifteen*   3:15

Number a sheet of paper from 1 to 9. Write each time below.

1. 10:15
2. 8:04
3. 5:30

Use numbers and colons to write each time below. Remember that numbers are the same size as tall letters.

4. **ten minutes past seven**
5. **twenty minutes past one**
6. **quarter after eleven**

When you write the abbreviations **a.m.** and **p.m.**, use lower-case letters and periods.

Write the times below. Next to each time, write what you are usually doing at that time of day.

7. **7:00 a.m.**
8. **4:10 p.m.**
9. **8:15 p.m.**

Making a Schedule

Tanya and her family had to move to a new town. She decided to make a schedule of what she had to do for the week before she moved. To make the schedule, Tanya drew a box and some vertical lines on notebook paper.

Read Tanya's schedule below. Look at the size of the letters. The capital letters do not touch the top line, but the small letters are still half the size of the tall letters. This means the words are written in adult proportion.

Day	Things to Do	Time
Wed.	Dentist	3:30 p.m.
Thurs.	Dinner at Aunt Flossie's	5:30 p.m.
Fri.	Sleepover at Keisha's	6:30 p.m.
Sat.	Pizza lunch with Scouts	11:15 a.m.–12:45 p.m.
Sun.	Moving day	9:00 a.m.

On a sheet of paper, make a form like the one below. Copy Tanya's schedule in the form. Adjust the size of your handwriting to fit the space. Use adult proportion. Keep your small letters half the size of your tall letters.

Day	Things to Do	Time

Writing Addresses

Riki wrote a letter to her dad. She made sure she wrote the words and numbers clearly so the letter would reach her dad's mailbox. Study Riki's envelope and the tips below.

Include a return address.

RIKI FULTON
219 BURR OAK DR
LAFAYETTE IN 47901

MR MARK FULTON
1609 W TYLER ST
ROCHESTER IN 46975

Use all capital manuscript letters and no punctuation marks.

On a sheet of paper, draw an envelope about the size of the one above. Address the envelope using the information below.

Mailing address: Ray Chasing Hawk, 619 River Road, Yankton, SD 57078

Return address: Jon Hanson, 525 South Hill Road, Baltimore, MD 21230

Can another person read your envelope?

Writing a Postcard

When you write a postcard, your writing must fit into a small space. Look at the words in the postcard below. They are written smaller than usual. Sometimes tall letters are very close to letters with descenders, but they do not bump into each other.

Potawatomi Memorial Village

*April 27, 200_*

Hi Dan,
   See the wigwam on this card? I sat inside one just like it. An Indian storyteller told us about the tribe's heroes.
          Eduardo

DAN HOFFMAN
24 ELM ST APT 18
WHITTIER CA 90609

On your paper, draw a postcard about the size of the one above. Use it to copy Eduardo's postcard. Adjust your writing to fit the space. Make sure your tall letters do not bump into letters with descenders.

Look at the postcard you wrote. Do your tall letters and letters with descenders fit into their own spaces?

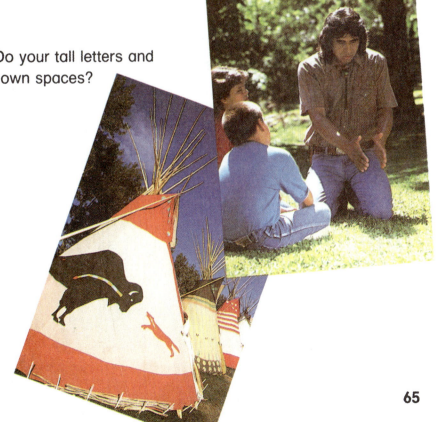

Writing Measurements

Most people abbreviate when they write measurements. Look at the chart below. Only the abbreviation for *inch* has a period. Also, only the abbreviation for *liter* has a capital.

inch	**in.**	ounce	**oz**
foot	**ft**	pound	**lb**
yard	**yd**	pint	**pt**
mile	**mi**	quart	**qt**
centimeter	**cm**	gallon	**gal**
meter	**m**	liter	**L**

Use the same abbreviation for singular and plural measurements.

Number a sheet of paper from 1 to 4. Rewrite the following measurements in cursive. Use abbreviations for the underlined words.

1. 15 <u>miles</u>
2. 26 <u>meters</u>
3. 8 <u>inches</u>
4. 1 <u>foot</u>

On a small piece of paper, copy the grocery list below. Write your numbers and tall letters twice as high as your small letters. Keep your lines straight.

5 lb rice
8 oz cottage cheese
1 gal milk
2 L apple juice

Writing a Recipe

What is the difference between the two words at the right? Of course, one is larger. Yet in each word the small letters are half the size of the tall letters. This shows that the letters are in correct proportion.

In the recipe card below, the ingredients are written in adult proportion. The capital letters do not touch the top line but the small letters are still half the size of the tall letters.

Meat Sauce for Spaghetti

½ lb ground beef
2 medium onions
16 oz can of whole tomatoes
6 oz can of tomato paste
1 teaspoon salt
1 teaspoon oregano

Use a lined index card or draw a box the size of an index card on your paper. Copy the recipe. Plan your space so that each ingredient fits on one line. Use adult proportion.

Look at what you have written. Circle a word that has tall letters and small letters. Did you make the small letters half the size of your tall letters?

Writing Ordinal Numbers

Ordinal numbers tell in what order or position things belong. They can be written as words or as numbers and letters combined. The ordinal numbers below are written in both ways. Notice that the numbers are not joined to the letters.

1st	first	6th	sixth
2nd	second	7th	seventh
3rd	third	8th	eighth
4th	fourth	9th	ninth
5th	fifth	10th	tenth

The phrases below are missing an ordinal number. Number your paper from 2 to 6. Show two ways that you can complete each phrase. Do not join numbers to letters. Use a different ordinal number for each phrase. The first one is done for you.

1. **made it on the ____ try**

   5th   fifth

2. **won ____ place**

   ____

3. **played ____ base**

   ____

4. **practiced it for the ____ time**

   ____

5. **sat in the ____ row**

   ____

6. **climbed to the ____ floor**

   ____

Join lower-case letters whenever you write in cursive. Remember that some capital cursive letters are connected to the lower-case letters that follow them.

Carla and her friends organized some games for the younger children in the neighborhood. She wrote a list to show how each child placed in each game. On a sheet of paper, copy Carla's list for Maurice. Join your letters correctly.

Game	Score	Place
Button in the Box	100	1st
Jump-rope Contest	22	4th
Beanbag Toss	8	6th

Fun with Handwriting: *Calligraphy*

The message above is written in calligraphy, a style of handwriting that is very beautiful. People use calligraphy to communicate and to express their feelings at the same time.

People began to do calligraphy in China about two thousand years ago. It was used to decorate books, letters, buildings, and works of art. Calligraphy is still popular today.

People learn to do calligraphy in the same way you learn handwriting—by practicing strokes on lined paper. Look at the strokes and letters below.

You can be very inventive when you use calligraphy. Here is one way calligraphers show off their skill.

The instructions below tell what you need to begin learning calligraphy. Copy the two paragraphs on another sheet of paper. Use manuscript or cursive handwriting.

To begin to learn calligraphy, you need a black felt-tip marker and lined paper with dotted midlines.

Hold your pen at a 45-degree angle so that the pen points over your shoulder. Practice writing an X on your paper. Always hold the marker in the same position. Do not press hard. If you hold the pen correctly, the X will be thick in one direction and thin in the other. Look at this example.

Are you interested in learning more about calligraphy? In a library, you'll find books that show how to practice strokes, letters, and designs. You'll also see more beautiful examples of how people use calligraphy.

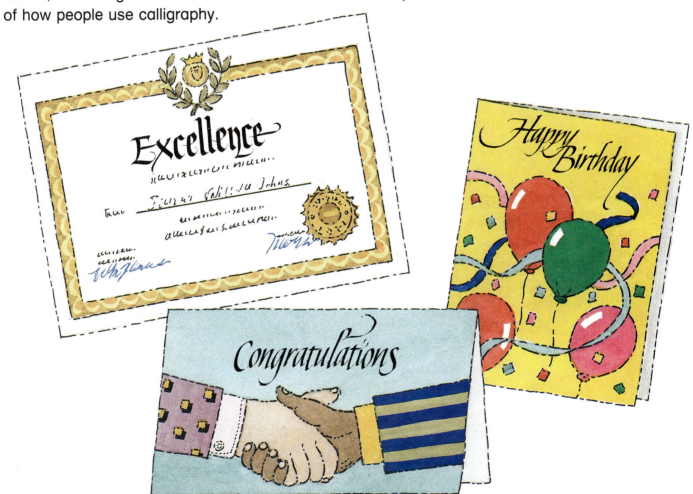

Fun with Handwriting: Riddles

Have you heard any colorful riddles or jokes lately? Here are a few that might brighten your day. Number your paper from 1 to 6. After you find the answers, write them on a separate sheet of paper. Use either manuscript or cursive handwriting.

Burple!

1. If all of the cars in the U.S. were pink, what would we have?

2. What was purple and conquered the world?

3. Which burns longer, a red or a green candle?

Alexander the Grape!

A pink carnation!

4. Hey! That's a strange pair of socks you have on—one red and the other green.

5. Eat your spinach. It will put color into your cheeks.

6. If buttercups are yellow, what color are hiccups?

Neither one. Both of them burn shorter.

Yes, and the funny thing about it is that I have another pair at home exactly like this one!

Who wants green cheeks?

Letter, Word, and Sentence Spacing

What would happen if your teacher asked your class to sit in groups of three? Everyone would probably sit so there were small spaces between students and larger spaces between groups. Even spacing is important in handwriting as well.

Marta and Lawrence both wrote compositions about their heritage. On a sheet of paper, copy Marta's first paragraph below in cursive. Make even spaces between letters. Leave a larger space between words. Make more space between sentences than between words in a sentence.

My mother talks to me in Spanish. It's easier for me to speak English, but I usually answer her in Spanish. Mom says it's important to learn the language of my heritage. I think, sí, it's a good idea.

Did you make even spaces between letters? Did you leave enough space between words and sentences?

On a separate sheet of paper, write Lawrence's first paragraph below in cursive. Use correct spacing.

Cowboys, horses, and the Old West—that's what I like. Did you know that more than one-fourth of the cowboys were African American? My favorite black cowboy was Nat Love. People nicknamed him "Deadwood Dick."

Did you make even spaces between letters? between words? between sentences?

Timed Writing

Dwayne received a call from his softball coach at the beginning of the spring season. Read what the coach said to Dwayne.

"Hi, Dwayne. This is Mr. Duff, your softball coach. I'm calling all the players to tell them that we'll start practice on Monday. That's April 22. We'll practice every Monday and Wednesday afternoon from 5:30 to 6:30 at Weiss Park. If you need to call me, my number is 555-9023. Okay?"

Use these tips when you take a telephone message.
- Ask the caller to wait until you get a pencil and paper.
- Write important information such as name, date, time, and place. Use manuscript or cursive, whichever is faster.
- Ask the caller to repeat information that you aren't sure of.

Write the message from Mr. Duff on another sheet of paper. Time your writing. Use a clock, a timer, or have a friend time you. Stop writing when four minutes are up.

Now read what you wrote. Did you write the dates, times, and numbers correctly?

Writing an Announcement

Suppose you wanted to tell people about a coming event. How would you do it? You could write an announcement. An announcement tells *what* the event is, *when* it will take place, and *where* it will be.

where and when ▶

what ▶

Veteran's Day Celebration

Stop by the Media Center during the week of November 7 between 11:00 A.M. and 1:00 P.M. to join in the celebration of Veteran's Day. Our librarians, Mrs. Cortez and Mr. Phillips, have gathered together an impressive collection of informative books, photographs, and videos dedicated to this subject. Please come and honor the men and women who bravely serve our country as members of the military. Refreshments will be served.

Imagine that you want to announce a special event such as an open house at your school, a concert, or a talent show. Write an announcement about it on a separate sheet of paper. Use manuscript handwriting. Slant all your letters in the same direction.

Look over your announcement. Do your letters all slant in the same direction? Are they the correct size?

76 Maintaining Manuscript

Writing Punctuation Marks

Punctuation marks help you understand the meaning of the cartoon. In fact, punctuation marks add meaning to everything you read and write. It is important to know how to form punctuation marks and where to place them. Number your paper from 1 to 9. Copy the punctuation marks below.

1. period   .
2. question mark   ?
3. exclamation mark   !
4. apostrophe   '
5. comma   ,
6. quotation marks   " "

When you write contractions in cursive, do not join the letters on either side of the apostrophe. Copy the words below.

7. *can't*   8. *doesn't*   9. *wouldn't*

On your paper, copy the paragraph in cursive. Make sure you place the punctuation marks in the correct position. Slant them in the same direction as the rest of your handwriting.

When I smelled smoke, I didn't wait. I called the emergency number. "My house is on fire!" I said. Then I went outside to wait for help. How's that for quick thinking?

Write your own sentence on your paper. Use as many punctuation marks as you can.

Writing a Journal Entry

People write in journals to keep their own record of what they think, feel, see, and do. It is important to write legibly so that later you can read what you wrote.

Just as your journal is personal, your handwriting is also personal. You show your own style in the way you slant your letters. You may slant your letters to the right or to the left. You may write straight up-and-down. Keep the same slant when you write.

Read what Khanh wrote in his journal about facing new experiences in America.

May 16, 200__

Today at the mall I saw a little boy who was afraid to get on the escalator. He reminded me of myself when I first came here from Vietnam. I was scared of escalators, the kids at school, and just about everything. Now I'm used to living here—well, almost.

On a sheet of paper, write a short list of things that little children might be afraid of. Slant your letters in the same direction.

On a separate sheet of paper, write your own journal entry about something you wouldn't mind sharing. Choose a memory, your feelings, or what you did on a certain day. Some of the words below may help you start. Remember to slant all your letters in the same direction.

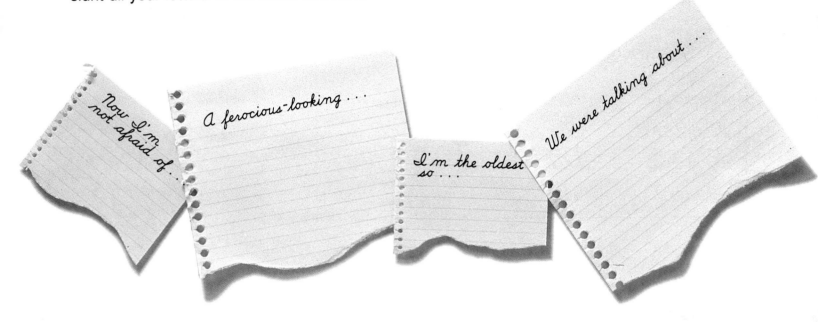

Now I'm not afraid of...

A ferocious-looking...

I'm the oldest so...

We were talking about...

Writing Proper Nouns

Begin proper nouns with capital letters. Remember that some capital cursive letters are not joined to the letters that follow. Look at the capital letters in the names below. They are not joined to the letters that follow them.

Lunchroom Helpers for January		
Brenda	Hannah	Tran
Delia	Oscar	Val
Frank	Pablo	Wayne
Gerry	Stacy	Xavier

Number a sheet of paper from 1 to 15. Write each name in the list.

1. _____
2. _____
3. _____
4. _____
5. _____
6. _____
7. _____
8. _____
9. _____
10. _____
11. _____
12. _____

Begin titles such as Mrs., Ms., Mr., Miss, and Dr. with capital letters. If the title is also an abbreviation, end it with a period. Write the titles and names of the teachers below.

13. **Dr. Carol Adamek**

14. **Mr. Martin Red Cloud**

15. **Mrs. Regina Fuller**

Write your name. Give yourself a title.

Making Signs

Justin's grandfather taught him to make wooden signs. Justin decided to make some signs with his friends' names on them and give them to his friends as gifts. First he wrote the names large on strips of paper. When he made the wooden signs, he enlarged the names even more.

REBECCA

JOEY

NIEVES

MR. ROH

CHARLIE

DELORES

On a sheet of paper, draw boxes about the size of the ones above. Then write the names in the boxes. Use manuscript writing. Adjust your writing to fit the space.

Maintaining Manuscript

Writing Dates

The days of the week begin with capital letters. A period follows the abbreviation of each.

On a sheet of paper, draw a form like the one below. Write abbreviations for the days of the week in the form. Adjust your writing so that it fits the space. Remember to write in a straight line.

Days of the Week

| Sun. | Mon. | Tues. | Wed. | Thurs. | Fri. | Sat. |

The months also begin with capital letters. So do their abbreviations. Notice that May, June, and July do not need to be abbreviated because they are short words. Look at the months below. Draw a form like the one shown and then write the months in it.

Months of the Year

Jan.	Feb.	Mar.
Apr.	May	June
July	Aug.	Sept.
Oct.	Nov.	Dec.

Number your paper from 1 to 3. Below are names of three Olympic stars and the dates they won medals. Write the dates in cursive. When you write a date, put a comma between the day and the year. Slant numbers in the same direction that you slant letters.

Michael Phelps   Aug. 21, 2004

Lisa Fernandez   Aug. 23, 2004

Mia Hamm   Aug. 28, 2004

On your paper, write some dates that are important to you.

Keeping an Assignment Book

Keeping an assignment book is a good way to remember your daily homework and future projects. You don't have to write in complete sentences. Form your letters and numbers correctly so you can easily read what you have to do.

On a sheet of paper, draw a form like the one below. Imagine that you must do the assignments listed on the chalkboard. Use the information to fill out the form. Concentrate on closing letters **a, d,** and **o.** Keep your lines straight as you write.

> *Tues., Apr. 2 – Today's Assignments*
> In social studies, read pages 200-204; draw a sod house on a prairie. Due Wed., Apr. 3.
> In reading, finish reading *Teammates*. Due tomorrow.
> In math, work on the Native American Design Project. Due Fri., Apr. 26.

Name			Today's Date
Subject	**Today's Assignments**		**Date Due**

Timed Writing

Lyman decided to take notes during a class discussion about deserts. Read below what a few students in his class said.

"Rain doesn't fall very often."

"I wish I could go camping in the desert."

"Deserts look dull brown, but after a heavy rain flowers bloom."

"Some plants store their own water—like the cactus. One cactus is called the saguaro."

Use these tips when you take notes.
- Use manuscript or cursive handwriting, whichever is faster for you.
- Write down important facts and information.
- Use phrases or short sentences.

What did the students say about the desert that would be important to remember? On another sheet of paper, write notes about that information. Time your writing. Use a clock, a timer, or have a friend time you. Stop writing when four minutes are up.

Now read what you wrote. Can you understand what you wrote? Did you write important facts?

Fun with Handwriting: Fantastic Letters

Dana stared at some letters for a while. Suddenly she imagined that they turned into something else! What did letter **g** become?

If you stared at capital **M** for a while, what could it turn into?

Let your imagination go. Look at the capital and lower-case letters in the frame below. Choose one or several letters. Write them upside down, sideways, or in any direction. Use another sheet of paper to draw a frame and create your design or picture.

Write a title or caption in the bottom of the frame.

85

Writing Titles

The meaning of the first sentence at the right would be confusing if the title did not have capitals and quotation marks.

When you write the titles of books and poems, capitalize the first word and all the important words. Put quotation marks around the title of poems. Also, underline the titles of books.

Now can you find the title of a book in the second sentence?

When I baby-sat for Donny, I read "I Called to the Wind" to him and he fell right to sleep.

I'm sending you Stone Fox for helping me pack all my books when I moved.

Number a sheet of paper from 1 to 4. Write the book title below. Remember to underline book titles.

1. *Nadia the Willful*

Write the title of the poem below. Put quotation marks around the title of a poem.

2. *"Our Hamster's Life"*

Copy the following sentences in cursive. When you come to the title of a book or poem, rewrite it so that it is correct.

3. **don't yell at me is a poem about how kids feel.**

4. **Remember Adan's trip to Puerto Rico in the book yagua days?**

Writing a List of Favorite Books

The students in Julia's class wrote lists of books they would recommend to their classmates. They drew small pictures next to the titles.

Number a sheet of paper from 1 to 3. Then look at the list of books and the pictures below. Find titles that match the pictures. Write the titles on your paper. Underline each title. Write small to fit each title on one line.

The Young Black Stallion   **The Phantom Tollbooth**   **My Side of the Mountain**

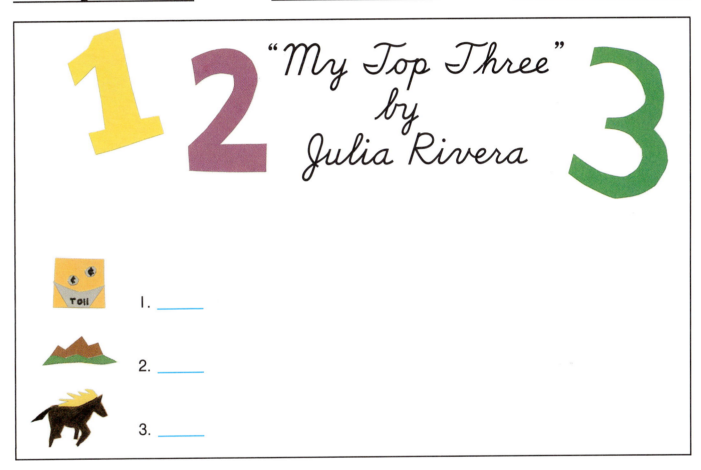

Write the title of a book you would recommend to someone. You may draw a picture to go with it.

87

Writing a Poem

Look at the following poem by Shel Silverstein. Each line begins with a capital letter, whether or not it begins a sentence. Many poems are written in this form.

Copy the poem in cursive on a sheet of paper. You may have to write smaller than usual to fit each line of the poem on one writing line. Capitalize the first word in each line.

MAGICAL ERASER

She wouldn't believe
This pencil has
A magical eraser.
She said I was a silly moo,
She said I was a liar too,
She dared me prove that it was true,
And so what could I do—
I erased her!

Now look at the poem below. It does not look like "Magical Eraser." Can you recognize the shape of this poem? That's right—it's a moon. The shape of the poem helps us picture the idea just as the words do.

On a sheet of paper, copy the poem "Moon String." Use manuscript handwriting.

Moon String

**Tonight
    the moon
        is a silver
          string
            stitched
              in a sky
                of black.
              A curve
            of white
            so fragile
          and thin
        a passing
      cloud
    could tear
its light.**

Beverly J. Letchworth

Maintaining Manuscript

Making a Poster

LaToya's science class studied how pollution affects the environment. They decided to make posters encouraging others to fight pollution. LaToya made one about recycling.

First she worked out her ideas on a sheet of paper, as shown below. Her paper is the same shape as the posterboard, but smaller. Notice how large she wrote the words. When LaToya makes the poster itself, she will enlarge the words to fit the size of the poster.

On another sheet of paper, copy LaToya's poster or plan one of your own. Use manuscript writing. You may want to use your poster plan to make a real poster. If you do, adjust your writing to fit the large posterboard.

Writing a Thank-you Note

When you write a thank-you note in neat, legible handwriting, you show that you really mean what you say.

Your handwriting will be more legible if you always join lower-case letters when you write in cursive. Remember that some capital letters are joined to the lower-case letters that follow them, while others are not.

Study Marina's thank-you note.

> May 24, 200_
>
> Dear Uncle Alex,
>   Thank you for lending me your Spartan soldier doll and the worry beads. No one else brought Greek things for "Many Cultures Day" at our school! May I keep them until you visit us in July?
>
>   Your niece,
>   Marina

On a sheet of paper, draw a space about the size of the one below. Copy the thank-you note in cursive. Remember to join lower-case cursive letters. Include the date, salutation, and closing.

Timed Writing

Gail just moved to a new city. She asked Rosa for directions to the park where they planned to meet after school. Rosa was in a hurry so Gail had to write quickly. Read the directions below.

"From the front of school, go left on Jackson Street to the third street. Turn right on Ninth Street. Go two blocks. You'll see the park on the left side of the street. It's at Ninth and Deming streets."

Use these tips when someone gives you directions.
- Use manuscript or cursive handwriting, whichever is faster for you.
- Write down important names and numbers.
- Ask the person to repeat anything you aren't sure of.

Imagine that you are Gail. Write the directions on another sheet of paper. Time your writing. Use a clock, a timer, or have a friend time you. Stop writing when two minutes are up.

Now read what you wrote. Could you follow the directions? Did you write the names and numbers?

Writing a Science Test

Good handwriting helps you do well on science tests. It makes your words easy to read.

Getting Ready
- Read each test question carefully.
- Study any graphs or charts that are part of the question.
- Be sure you understand what to do.

Reading a Graph
- Look at the data results on the graph.
  Find the information that the question asks about.

- Be sure that you answer every part of the question.
- Use your best handwriting.
  Letters should not be too close together or too far apart.
  Letters should be the correct size and proportion to fit the space.

Tomato ^plants need more than two hours of sun per day. I used ordered pairs on the graph.

- Review and edit your writing. Use proofreading marks to make changes or erase carefully and rewrite.

93

Daniel answered a question using the graph below.

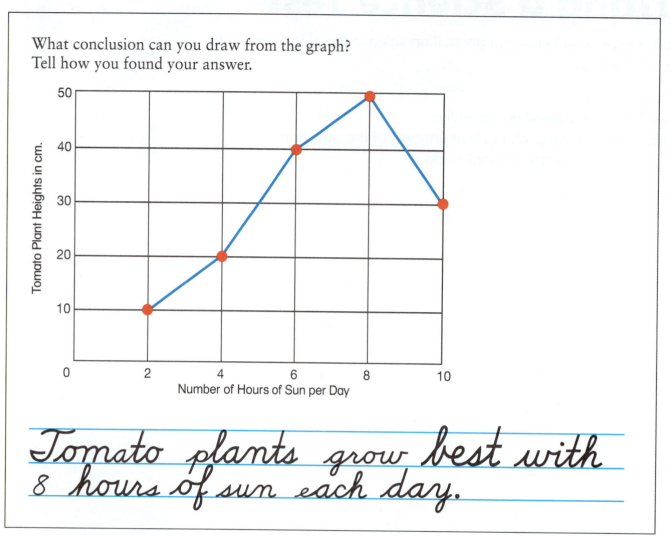

What conclusion can you draw from the graph?
Tell how you found your answer.

Tomato plants grow best with 8 hours of sun each day.

Look at how Daniel answered the question.
- Did he answer every part of the question?
- Are his letters the correct size and proportion to fit the space?

Yes No

Which letters or words are not the correct size? Write them on a separate piece of paper. What part of the question is not answered? Write an answer.

On a separate piece of paper, answer a question using the graph shown below.

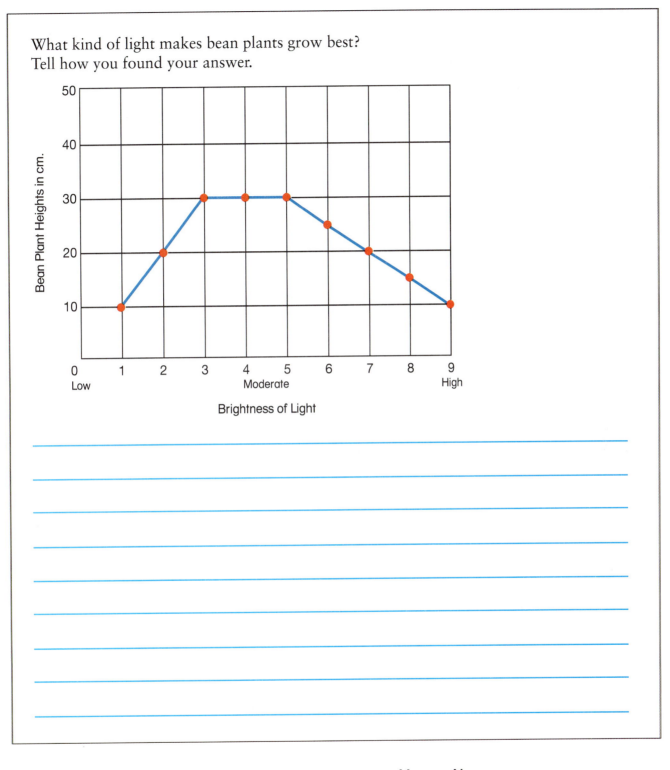

What kind of light makes bean plants grow best?
Tell how you found your answer.

Check your handwriting.

Number your paper from 1 to 3. Write your answers.
1. Did you answer every part of the question?
2. Are your letters the correct size and proportion to fit the space?
3. Did you fix mistakes carefully?

Yes   No

Circle the word you wrote best.

Index

Abbreviations
  addresses, 64, 65
  days and months, 82
  measurements, 66
  time, 62
  titles of people, 80
Addresses, 64, 65
Adjusting handwriting
  adult proportion, 33, 63, 67
  size, 9, 32, 34, 65, 81, 87, 88, 90
  tall letters and descenders, 32, 55, 65
  without writing lines, 9, 10, 32, 34, 64, 65, 83
Announcement, 76
Assignment, 22
Assignment book, 83
Awards, 60
Bookplate, 9
Business card, 34
Calligraphy, 70–71
Capitalization
  of abbreviations, 66
  of addresses, 64, 65
  of book and poem titles, 86–87
  of days and months, 82
  of first words in poems, 88
  of proper nouns, 80
  of titles of people, 80
Common stroke letter groups, cursive
  aA, dD, cC, 26
  eE, jJ, pP, 14
  gG, yY, qQ, 28
  lL, hH, kK, 12
  nN, mM, xX, 27
  oO, wW, bB, 37
  sS, rR, fF, 49
  tT, iI, uU, 13
  vV, zZ, 48
Crossword puzzle, 35
Cursive handwriting joining strokes
  capital letters, 12, 13, 14, 26, 27, 28, 37, 48, 49, 80
  sidestroke, 38, 40, 50
  uphill, 12
Dates, 82
Directions, 92
Evaluating handwriting, 10, 16, 17, 18, 20, 21, 22, 24, 25, 30, 31, 32, 34, 40, 41, 42, 43, 44, 46, 47, 52, 53, 56, 58, 59, 64, 65, 67, 73, 74, 75, 76, 84, 92. See also Legibility
Evaluation, 17, 31, 41, 53. See also Legibility
Fantastic letters, 85
Fun with handwriting, 36, 60, 70–71, 72, 85

Joining sidestroke letters, 38, 40, 50
Journal entries, 46, 78–79
Legibility
  letter, word, and sentence spacing, 10, 19, 32, 55, 65, 73–74, 81
  letter form, 15, 17, 18, 29, 30, 31, 38, 39, 40, 41, 42–43, 51, 52, 53, 83, 88, 91
  letter size and proportion, 9, 16, 18, 32–33, 34, 39, 40, 52, 63, 65, 67, 88, 90
  letter slant, 19, 54–55, 77, 78–79, 82
Letters
  cursive
    aA, 26; bB, 37; cC, 26; dD, 26; eE, 14; fF, 49; gG, 28; hH, 12; iI, 13; jJ, 14; kK, 12; lL, 12; mM, 27; nN, 27; oO, 37; pP, 14; qQ, 28; rR, 49; sS, 49; tT, 13; uU, 13; vV, 48; wW, 37; xX, 27; yY, 28; zZ, 48
  manuscript, 6–7
List, 66, 69, 78, 87
Literature, 23, 45, 57, 93
Manuscript writing
  letter review, 6–7
  using, 9, 10, 34, 35, 60, 64, 65, 76, 81, 89, 90
Measurements, 66, 67
Messages, 10, 44, 75
Name cards, 32
Note-taking, 56, 84
Nouns, proper, 80
Numbers, 8
  in addresses, 64, 65
  in measurements, 66, 67
  ordinal, 68–69
  in time, 62, 63
Ordinal numbers, 68–69
Poems, writing, 88–89
Postcard, 65
Poster, 90
Practical Applications
  addresses, 64, 65
  announcement, 76
  assignment, 22
  assignment book, 83
  awards, 60
  bookplate, 9
  business card, 34
  calligraphy, 70–71
  dates, 82
  directions, 92
  fantastic letters, 85
  journal entries, 46, 78–79
  list, 66, 69, 78, 87
  measurements, 66, 67

  messages, 10, 44, 75
  name cards, 32
  note-taking, 56, 84
  poems, 88–89
  postcard, 65
  poster, 90
  recipe, 67
  riddles, 72
  schedule, 63
  show-off writing, 36
  signs, 81
  thank-you note, 91
  time, 62, 63
  titles, 42, 86–87
Practice, 15, 29, 39, 51
Proofreading, 20–21, 24, 25, 46, 47, 58, 59, 94, 95
Proofreading marks, 20–21
Proper nouns, 80
Punctuation marks
  apostrophe, 77
  colon, 62
  comma, 8, 77, 82
  exclamation mark, 77
  period, 77, 80, 82
  question mark, 77
  quotation marks, 77, 86
  underlining, 86–87
Recipe, 67
Review, 16, 30, 40, 52
Riddles, 72
Schedule, 63
Show-off writing, 36
Signs, 81
Test Preparation
  Writing a Language Arts Test, 23–25
  Writing a Math Test, 45–47
  Writing a Language Arts Test, 57–59
  Writing a Science Test, 93–95
Thank-you note, 91
Thinking skills
  classifying, 87, 94
  fact versus opinion, 84
  summarizing, 22, 44, 56, 75, 84, 92
Timed writing, 22, 44, 56, 75, 84, 92
Time, 62, 63
Titles, 86
  of books and poems, 42, 86–87
  of people, 80
Writing process
  drafting, 25, 47, 59, 95
  presenting, 25, 47, 59, 95
  prewriting, 24, 46, 58, 94
  proofreading, 20–21, 24, 25, 46, 47, 58, 59, 94, 95
  revising, 25, 47, 59, 95